YOU KNOW ME

YOU KNOW ME

LKP

You Know Me Records

Contents

Dedicated to
those who are
not afraid
of the dark...

First Printing, 2024

I

THE END

if you loved me
I wouldn't be
bruising my knees
begging for you
not to leave

the taste of my tears
the sight of my fears
the ache of my years

...

I carry with me
these souvenirs

my haiku for you
but I stop it halfway through
words I can't undo

you and I
are not the same,
you grew up with love
I grew up with shame

...

home to home
bone to bone
so I hold
the skeleton alone

would you rather
feel nothing at all
or feel everything
and fall?

sicario
look at
what you've done,
mi amor
love is
not a gun

cold marble floor
meets warm crimson blood,
the irony
of insanity

I remember
you read me everyday
then one day
you choked on words to say
the beginning of your line
started with just an
'okay'
I could feel the space
between us
you became
the perfect cliché

poppy seeds
aren't enough to feed
the hunger pain
inside of you

...

poppy tears flow
where hurt grows
so you water it
until you feel no more

I wander through
the valley of somber
searching for a song
to conquer,
my knees
so dirty and weak
as they cover
my mouth to speak,
rip my gift
from my throat
sip and strip
my only hope

put the bottle down
take a look around
what do you see?
broken glass
broke like the last
time you held me

passion into obsession,
aggression into confession
...
the growth of
the undead rose

liquor turns
to love
a sober day
turns to none
drinking to fill up
emptiness in a cup

...

it burns
on the way down
but in that hell
you feel found

swallow
the pill
in order
to kill
loneliness,
start to
undress
sins you
confess
praying you will

I bite
my tongue
until
I taste
blood,
it is
better
than
the taste
of
unrequited love

there is
nothing
more
distracting
than the
thought of
someone else
so
I burn
every
last piece of
my mind
until
the thought of you melts

isn't it ironic
he sells
a rock
to buy
more rocks
to wear
on his neck,
isn't it ironic
he pays
a price
for eyes
but the
price is
on his head

a
beautiful song
comforts me
in my
ugliest hour,
soothing
my weakness
the melody
holds
power

I never
loved you
anyway
I tell
myself
as
I dig
your grave

you're
the reason
I'm alive
and you're
the reason
I'm deprived
...
you are
the devil
in disguise

I
carved
your name
into my
wrist,
a reminder
of pain
that can't
be
fixed

after
the curtains
close
I'm all alone,
with an echo
of applause
but no one to call
my own

you
held my
beating
heart
in your
hand,
then asked me
why
I couldn't
stand

cigarettes
in the rain
are pointless,
like love
on the brain
it's heartless

in time, nothing hurts

...

nothing hurts, in time

I inherited
your eyes
your nose
and an obsession for control
~ letters to my mother

you
are
the most
breathtaking,
heartbreaking
poem
I will
ever
write

poetry
is
not dead,
it hangs
from the
brain
of a
scattered head

she
wanders
the street
at night
in bloody
heels
and a dress
that's tight
...
she's calling
for help
but you
just drive
if only
you knew
how she's
feeling inside

she chases
her cake
with a
glass
of 1942,
the taste
of her past
and lips
she once
knew

the
for you
page
is a
drug
they take,
doped up
on dopamine
and fifteen
seconds
of fame

she sells
love at
the club
every
Friday night,
she's dancing
for you
with tears
in her
eyes

dear
almost lover,
have you
found another?
I have yet
to recover
since I
met you
that summer

...

P.S.
if you
still wonder
I have
the same number
sincerely, lkp

welcome to
Hollywood
the place
everyone plays
a role,
wishing upon
a star
to have
anything
but a soul

I dared
the devil
to kiss
my lips,
my body
burned
for his
fingertips

the difference
between
love
and I,
is one of us
lives
and the other
dies

living
my life
through a
blue screen,
all eyes
on me
but never
seen

I was
an ace
at giving space,
you were
a pro
at letting go
...
there is
no winning
playing games
for a living

a scar
on my
thigh,
a touch
makes me
cry
...
burning
alive,
breaking
inside

afraid
to take
so I don't
give,
afraid
to die
so I don't
live
...
the irony
is killing
me

behind the
scenes
is politics,
this industry
is lies
and tricks

...

pay the
price for
the fame,
sacrifice
your own
name

there was a little girl
with long black hair,
she had a mother
so beautiful they'd stare

...

as the girl grew
older and older,
her mothers envy
grew colder
and colder

...

she would lock
the girl away
and starve her
for days,
and hold her
in a way
that left her
arms grey

...

there was a little girl
with long black hair,
she had a voice
so beautiful she'd share

I keep
the blinds
closed
and don't
let anyone in,
I grab
a bottle
and sing
to sad violins

...

light
a cigarette
and fall asleep,
wake me up
when I'm
burning in peace

you left
me
out in
the cold,
with nothing
but your
words
to hold

...

I froze
to death
to keep
you warm,
and you
moved on
to your
next storm

brokenhearted
and waiting tables,
in the city
of lost angels

...

daydreaming
of waking famous,
night walking
with the a-list

...

take it down
feel it now
will I
make it
in the city
of lost angels,
hear the doubt
get me out
will I
make it
in the city
of lost angels

homesick
with
no home,
someplace
I'm not
alone
...
lovesick
with
no love,
someone
I'm thinking
of

why are we
so afraid to cry?
drown ourselves
until we're empty inside

...

bury it
six feet under
there's no way out,
fading into
nothingness
the fatal drought

cursing
each other
until our
teeth are black,
stained from
the words
we can't
take back

...

a broken
mirror
with your
face,
and a
broken daughter
who's taken
your place

...

we accept
the love
we once
observed,
not the
love we
thought
we deserved

you are
not my
mother,
you are
the mother
of suffer
...
you are
the monster
that takes
life when
it's feeding,
you are
the demon
that pours
salt when
I'm bleeding
...
sadistic
in your ways
you always
play victim,
narcissistic
abuse
you abuse
the system

fragile
like a
porcelain
doll,
breaking
apart
to stay
small

...

placed
in a
case
for display,
a plastic
world
made her
this way

pretty
hurts,
like a
rose

...

a
beautiful
curse,
the more
envy
grows

...

picking
my petals
until I
fall,
perfection
means
nothing
at all

hanging
from
the ceiling,
losing
every
feeling
...
a life
without
dreaming
is
a life
without
meaning

witches
never
burn,
ghosts
always
return
...
things
that keep
me up
at night,
are the
things
that never
bite

this
sadness
is not
mine,
still I
hold it
and say
I'm fine
...
made
from
a broken
line,
a daughter
with a
broken
spine

he is
the first
since
my
last,
but
in the
future
he is
my past

if I'm
a wound
you're
the salt,
ice cold
heart
and it's
all your
fault

you held
me
so tight
my body
turned
blue
and said
sometimes
I hate you
means
I love you
too

girls in LA
are not
like me,
starving
for fame
and living
for free

...

staring
into
a broken
vanity,
the cost
of beauty
is her
sanity

can you
feel my
shame
when I'm
wrapped
around your
skin?
I say
his
name
and
pretend
you are
him

e.go /ˈēgō/
the starving demon
you keep on feeding

anx·i·ety \aŋ-ˈzī-ə-tē\
the feeling
of nothing
and everything
at the same time

art /ärt/
the expression
of my depression

I am
only
known
when
I am
alone

...

come
too close
and you
will see,
now
you don't
even
know me

II

THE BEGINNING

as long as it's got a spark,
it's always going to light

some
call me
a witch
others
call me
enchanting

I'ved loved you
all nine lives,
more and more
every time

I feel your warmth
in the rain,
I see you dancing
in my flame,
you stay with me
I wear your name,
someday we'll be
together again

remember me
and the words I speak,
tell my story
memento mori

translating words
into art,
a love language
of the heart

her silhouette
was art,
with every curve
she fell apart

...

traced her frame
until she came,
paint her smooth
my poetic muse

you melted
on my tongue
and breathed
into my lungs,
we both
came undone
we both
became one

I
am the
work of
art
that
works
for art

when
you heard
his voice
for the
first time
you knew
you were home,
he wrapped you
in his
soft
words
and you let
yourself
go

his eyes
were bluer
than the
clearest sky,
maybe
that's why
she loved
to fly

she belonged
to the world
until
she made her own,
her mind
was the creator
and her body
a home

the California
sun
touches
my hips,
a California
star
kisses
my lips

...

in his eyes
a familiar
gleam,
once upon
a Hollywood
dream

today
is the day
I take back
my power,
I am
no longer
a delicate
flower

...

I am
the tree
that stands still
in a tornado,
I am
the rain
that floods
until there's a rainbow

...

I am
blue and
I am red,
I am
the start and
I am the end

the ocean
in her eyes
and a
heart of
gold,
the forest
in her hair
and a
hand to
hold
...
in this place
together,
always
and forever

I am
a star,
always
burning
...
you are
the world,
always
turning
...
in the
sky
we both
are searching

home is
where the
art is,
music
where my
heart is

a spark
to
flames,
a body
to
remains
...
from
the ashes
she will
rise,
a
girl
on fire
never dies

life
is the
art of
trying,
fear
is the
art of
dying

things
that make
you rich
are free,
a little
life is
poetry

I love you
more than
words
can say,
you are
my night
and you are
my day
...
I'll be
yours
until we're
grey,
so hold me
tonight
and tell me
you'll stay

there is
no body
like
your body,
be the
warmth
that you
embody
~ letters to myself

I grew up
in the trees,
hiding
from the
winter
breeze

...

a small
place
with small
things
and
the comfort
that familiar
brings

love /ləv/
is not a size or prize,
it cannot be bought or taught;
it is real and it is free,
it can be you and it can be me

now
you
know
me
...

LKP is a Canadian poet and musician originally from Vanderhoof, British Columbia. She writes dark, melancholic poetry that is authentic and relatable. When she's not writing, she can be found singing, practising yoga, or wandering through nature. LKP currently resides in Vancouver, British Columbia with her partner and cat, where she is hard at work on her debut EP.

Printed in the USA
CPSIA information can be obtained
at www.ICGtesting.com
LVHW011319260524
781307LV00004B/239